GARETH STEVENS
VITAL SCIENCE
Physical Science

ELECTRICITY AND MAGNETISM

by Steve Parker
Science curriculum consultant: Suzy Gazlay, M.A.,
science curriculum resource teacher

Please visit our Web site at: www.garethstevens.com
For a free color catalog describing Gareth Stevens Publishing's
list of high-quality books, call 1-800-542-2595 (USA)
or 1-800-387-3178 (Canada).
Gareth Stevens Publishing's fax: 1-877-542-2596

Library of Congress Cataloging-in-Publication Data available upon request from publisher.
Fax (877) 542-2596 for the attention of the Publishing Record Department.

ISBN-13: 978-0-8368-8085-4 (lib. bdg.)
ISBN-13: 978-0-8368-8094-6 (softcover)

This edition first published in 2007 by
Gareth Stevens Publishing
A Weekly Reader® Company
1 Reader's Digest Rd.
Pleasantville, NY 10570-7000 USA

This edition copyright © 2007 by Gareth Stevens, Inc.

Produced by Discovery Books
Editors: Rebecca Hunter and Amy Bauman
Designer: Barry Dwyer
Photo researcher: Rachel Tisdale

Gareth Stevens editorial direction: Mark Sachner
Gareth Stevens editors: Carol Ryback and Tea Benduhn
Gareth Stevens art direction: Tammy West
Gareth Stevens graphic design: Scott Krall and Dave Kowalski
Gareth Stevens production: Jessica Morris and Robert Kraus

Illustrations by Stefan Chabluk, Keith Williams
Photo credits: CFW Images: p. 5; CORBIS: pp. 4, 13 (Paul A. Souders), 20 (The Art Archive); Daimler
Chrysler: p. 39; Discovery Photo Library: cover & p. 29; Edison International: p. 37; Getty Images: pp. 7
(Richard Herrmann), 12 (Photodisc), 32 (Hulton Archive), 42 (Hulton Archive); Istockphoto.com: pp. 6
(Moritz van Hacht), 9 (David Raboin), 11 (Janne Ahro), 15, 16 (Kurt Gordon), 31 (Ralf Paprzycki), 40
(Simon Smith), 41 (Roberta Osborne); Newscast: pp. 35 (E-ON UK), 38 (Draklow Power Station); Philips:
p. 43; Science Photo Library: pp. 8 (AJ Photo/Hop Americain), 23 (Simon Fraser/Northumbria Circuits).

Printed in the United States of America

3 4 5 6 7 8 9 10 10 09 08

TABLE OF CONTENTS

Introduction 4

CHAPTER 1   The Nature of Electricity   6

CHAPTER 2   Static Electricity   12

CHAPTER 3   A Pathway for Electricity   16

CHAPTER 4   Mysterious Magnetism   24

CHAPTER 5   Electricity and Magnetism   28

CHAPTER 6   Generators and Grids   34

CHAPTER 7   Electronics   40

Glossary   44

Further Information   46

Index   48

Words that appear in the glossary are printed in **boldface** type the first time they appear in the text.

Cover: A crane uses electromagnetism to pick up and sort metal in a scrapyard.

Title page: In the control room at an electric power plant, an engineer monitors the generators and keeps track of how much electricity is produced.

Introduction

It won't be long before you use electricity or magnetism. And almost certainly you won't give it a second thought. As you get onto your computer or cell phone, relax in front of a TV or music system, ride in a car or bus or plane, flick on a hairdryer or blender or almost any other powered gadget—electricity and magnetism are there, obeying you in an instant.

Universal force

Electricity and magnetism are hard to separate. Where there's one, there is almost always the other. Electricity powers a lightbulb but also produces a tiny amount of magnetism around it. A loudspeaker or earphone is powered by electricity and has a strong magnet inside. An electric motor works only because it uses electricity to create magnetism inside itself, and the magnetism and electricity interact to cause the spinning movement of the motor.

Millions of city lights—here in Hong Kong—rely on the power of electricity to brighten our world and change night into day.

Electricity and magnetism are, in effect, two forms of the same force. This force is known as electromagnetism. Scientists view electromagnetism as one of the most basic, or fundamental, forces in the entire Universe. It is truly everywhere—even in deep space. The waves we can't see all around us, such as radio waves that bring us radio and television channels, and microwaves that carry phone calls and cook our food, consist of **electromagnetic** energy. So do the waves we can see as light. These may reach our eyes in an instant from the overhead lamp. They may also take billions of years to reach us from the most distant stars in deep space.

Magnets, like those pictured above, are amazingly useful and common. They often seem magical, with their mysterious attracting power almost like "invisible glue."

DANGER: MAGNETS!

Magnets—even small ones—should never be used around computers, magnetic tape (such as videotape), magnetic disks, or cards such as credit and security cards. A magnet can interfere with these items and destroy valuable data.

Everyday essential

Closer to home, electricity and magnetism are an essential part of modern life. Electricity is one of our most-used forms of energy—and it is readily available. Plug into a power outlet or pop in batteries (electrical **cells**), and you're ready to go. In fact, we rarely give these sources a thought—unless there's a power outage. The same could be said of some of the other forms of energy, such as heat and light. We take them for granted unless, for some reason, they are not available to us.

THE BIGGEST BLACKOUT

To date, the world's biggest power outage, or blackout, hit northeast North America on August 14, 2003. More than 60 million people lost their electricity. Subways and elevators halted; massive traffic jams developed. Big cities were paralyzed. That's how much we depend on electricity!

CHAPTER 1

The Nature of Electricity

We are familiar with electricity from power outlets and batteries (electrical cells). This electricity is produced, or generated, by human-made machines and chemicals. There is also electricity in nature. We see its effects whenever there's a thunderstorm. We can even see it in action in animals such as an electric eel or an electric ray.

We cannot see electricity. It is caused by the movements of certain particles—called **electrons**— within **atoms**, which are the tiniest units that make up all objects, substances, and matter. These particles and their movements are far too small to see. We can, however, see the effect of electricity. We can also hear the effects, and sometimes smell or feel them.

THE WORD *ELECTRICITY*

In ancient times, people knew that if they rubbed **amber** against certain materials such as fur, it attracted light objects such as feathers. Our words *electricity* and *electron* come from the old Greek name for amber, *elektron*.

Lightning

Lightning flashes are gigantic sparks of electricity that occur during a thunderstorm. The electrical energy builds up in clouds and suddenly jumps to the ground as lightning. This is known as an electrical **discharge**. With lightning, the discharge is visible. As it leaps, some of its energy turns into light, which we see. Some of it also turns into heat, which makes the air so hot that it expands faster than the speed of sound. We hear this as the boom of thunder.

Animal electricity

If you get too near an electric eel or electric ray, you may feel electricity. These fish have specialized muscles to produce strong surges, or shocks, of electricity. The

Lightning is a giant spark of electrical energy produced naturally in the thundercloud above. It leaps, or discharges, down to Earth and gives out heat, light, and sound.

WHAT IS SAINT ELMO'S FIRE?

In stormy weather, a dancing glow sometimes appears above and around tall or pointed objects such as ships' masts, church steeples, chimneys, and even aircraft wings. This eerie bluish-white light is called Saint Elmo's fire. It is natural electricity being discharged from these objects into the air, making it glow. This electricity has no heat, and it doesn't burn anything, but it may make a hissing sound.

As a thunderstorm builds, the air becomes increasingly charged with natural electricity. If the charge is particularly heavy, even the horns of cows may glow at their tips! Sailors took this light to be a good omen, or sign. They named it Saint Elmo's fire after the patron saint, or protector, of sailors. It is also known as a corona or point discharge.

surges are several times stronger than the electricity supply from an electrical outlet in your home. Electric rays and eels use their shocks to defend themselves and to stun their prey.

Electric rays and eels are not the only creatures that make electricity. All animals make it in their muscles, although only in tiny amounts. Some creatures can detect this animal electricity using sensors in their

THE "GHOSTLY FLAME"

"[A] ghostly flame which danced among our sails and later stayed like candlelights to burn brightly from the mast . . . When he appears, there can be no danger."

Christopher Columbus (1451–1506), Italian-born sailor and explorer, describes Saint Elmo's Fire.

Sharks can pick up tiny electrical pulses from the muscles of fish swimming nearby. Sensors in the pits on a shark's snout sense movement. They can sense extremely low levels of electricity.

Electricity and Magnetism

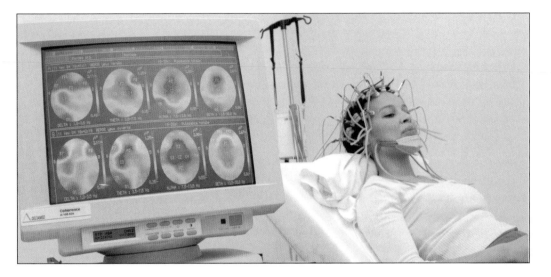

In an EEG, **electrode** pads stuck to the skin of the head pick up tiny electrical signals from the brain. Here, the signals are displayed on a computer "model" of the brain.

skin. The shark, for instance, has pores, known as ampullae of Lorenzini, in the skin over its snout. These pores sense electricity and tell the shark if there is a creature nearby, even in total darkness. Some fish can also detect electricity using tiny sensors in the stripe-like lateral line along each side of the body.

MEASURING ELECTRICITY

We measure the strength or pushing power of electricity in **volts**. A typical flashlight battery is 1.5 volts. An average car battery is 12 volts. Electricity from a standard wall outlet is 110 volts. Nerve signals in the human body are much smaller and measure about one-tenth (0.1) of a volt.

Human electricity

Like animal muscles, our muscles make electricity, too. Your beating heart is one such muscle. When it beats, its small electric pulses can be detected on the skin by sensor pads and displayed as a spiky line on a screen or paper roll. We call this an electrocardiogram (EKG or ECG). The pattern of lines shows the health of the heart.

Other parts of the body that use electricity are the nerves and brain. These parts of the **nervous system** send and receive information in the form of tiny pulses, known as nerve signals, millions every second. As with the heart, we can detect the brain's nerve signals using sensor pads on the head and display the signals as spiky lines. These lines are called an electroencephalogram, or EEG, and they represent "brain waves" of electricity. The EEG can help to reveal brain conditions such as epilepsy.

What is electricity?

We know that electricity is all around us in nature, and we use human-generated electricity in countless machines, gadgets, and equipment. But what exactly is electricity? To answer this question, we need to look at the tiniest unit of all substances—atoms. Everything is made of atoms. They are so small that the ink of the dot on this "i" contains billions and billions of atoms.

CONTROLLING BY THOUGHT

Some people have artificial limbs, called prostheses, which work by thought. Sensor pads on the skin of the head, or near the prosthesis, detect nerve signals from the wearer's body and send them to electric motors in the prosthesis, making it move.

An atom has several parts. Its center is called the **nucleus**. The nucleus consists of two types of particles, **protons** and **neutrons**. Protons have a form of energy called a positive charge. Neutrons are neutral, which means they have no charge,

Powerful electricity can easily kill. Wires carrying it must be held up high on towers, or buried safely in protective pipes.

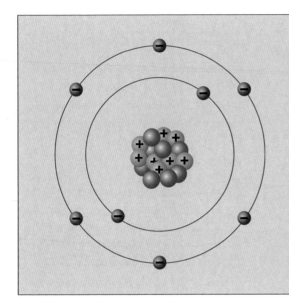

AN OXYGEN ATOM

An atom has electrons with negative charges (red), which circle its center or nucleus. The nucleus also contains protons with positive charges (green) and neutrons without a charge (blue). This atom, with eight of each kind of particle, represents the element oxygen.

so the nucleus as a whole has a positive charge. Around this nucleus whirl particles called electrons. Electrons have a negative charge. Normally, the electrons stay near their nucleus, going round and round in their orbits, like Earth and the other planets orbiting the Sun. The number of negatively charged electrons balances the number of positively charged protons, so, overall, the atom lacks any charge. It is neutral.

Electrons on the move

Sometimes, however, an electron gets knocked out of its orbit. This may happen if the atom receives extra energy, such as from light, movement, heat, or a chemical. Then the electron has enough energy to jump away. The energy has separated the negative electron from its atom. An atom that loses an electron has a positive charge. The process of electrons leaving their atoms is called the "separation of charge."

HOW FAST DO ELECTRONS MOVE?

When electricity flows through a wire, each individual electron does not move very far or very quickly. Each electron travels at a fraction of an inch (less than 1 millimeter) each second. This slight movement of billions of electrons has an immediate "ripple effect" along the wire, making it seem as if the electricity flows instantly. We say that electricity flows at the speed of light—186,000 miles (300,000 kilometers) per second.

Where does the electron go? It goes to another atom, which has also lost its electron. The positive charge of the atom that lost the electron and the negative charge of the free electron attract each other.

A flow of electricity

In an object, such as a metal wire, trillions of atoms are packed together. If they all receive energy at the same time, then each one loses an electron, which "hops" to the next atom. The new electron fills the gap left by that atom's own electron, which has hopped to the next atom . . . and so on. In this way, trillions of electrons hop from atom to atom along the wire. This mass movement, or flow of electrons is what we call electricity. Whatever energy form it was that started the flow of electrons has now been converted to electrical energy.

THALES OF MILETUS: FIRST STUDIES

One of the first people to study electricity and magnetism scientifically was Greek philosopher Thales of Miletus (circa 624–546 B.C.). As a merchant, he sailed widely, learned about navigation and geometry in Egypt, and came to believe that all things on Earth were originally water and would end up as water. None of Thales' writings survive. But reports from the time say that he knew about the naturally magnetic rock called lodestone, and he experimented with rubbing materials together to see how they attracted each other—what we now call **static electricity** (explained in Chapter 2).

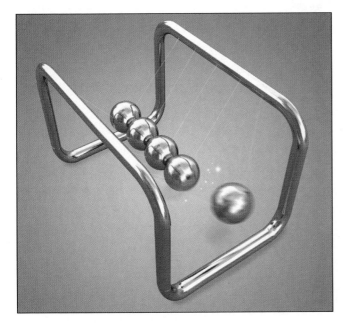

Moving electrons have a "knock on" effect as they jump from one atom to another in a wire. This is similar to the Newton's cradle toy, which shows how movement energy can be transferred from one ball to the next along the row.

Static Electricity

Electricity is a flow of electrons, hopping from one atom to the next. But this flow can happen in different ways. It may be steady, which we call electric current. Or it may happen suddenly and all at once as an electrical discharge. The kind of electricity that we call static electricity can suddenly move all at once, as an example of an electrical discharge.

Static electricity forms when electrons are removed from their atoms by a physical force, such as rubbing or contact with another substance. The negatively charged electrons remain separated from their positively charged nuclei, but they do not move far or flow. This separation of charged particles is called an electrostatic charge, or, more commonly, static electricity. This is the force that makes balloons stick to walls after rubbing them on your hair or clothing.

Static and lightning

Static electricity is also the reason that lightning forms. Tiny floating water droplets in the thundercloud swirl around and rub against each other, stripping electrons. The bottom part of the cloud builds up a negative charge. The top part of the cloud becomes positively charged. Eventually, the difference between the charges at the top and bottom of the cloud, or between the bottom of the cloud and the positively charged surface of Earth, become so great that some energy must be released. We see this as a lightning bolt in the cloud or discharging to the ground as a massive spark of jagged light.

Skyscrapers and other tall structures, like these in Chicago, Illinois, have large metal strips, or rods, to carry the electricity of a lightning strike safely into the ground.

This safe static electricity machine generates a static charge that travels all over the body and along every hair. So the hairs repel each other and the body, and become very "flyaway!"

Creating static electricity

Only certain substances and materials develop static charge when rubbed. They include many kinds of cloth, rubber, plastics, and glass. A familiar example is rubbing a party balloon on a wool dress or jacket. After a time, the balloon and the wool develop electrostatic charge. The balloon gains electrons and becomes negative. The wool loses them and becomes positive. Then, if the balloon is held up to a wall, it will stick. This

BENJAMIN FRANKLIN

U.S. scientist Benjamin Franklin (1706–1790) was also a printer, journalist, inventor, politician, and diplomat. At the age of twenty-seven, he wrote *Poor Richard's Almanac*, a collection of homespun sayings. At forty, he began experiments with electricity, which he called "electrical fluid." Wanting to prove his theory that lightning and electricity were the same thing, he once flew a kite in a thunderstorm. He attached a metal key to the string and flew the kite so that the key was suspended in open air. The electric charge passed down the damp string and caused a small spark between the key and Franklin's knuckle when he reached toward it. Although it proved his theory, it was an incredibly dangerous experiment. Later, in 1776, as America battled to be free from British control, Franklin helped write the Declaration of Independence.

THE LEYDEN JAR

One of the first devices to store electric charge was the Leyden jar, invented in 1745 in Leyden, Holland. It consisted of a glass jar partially filled with water and stopped with a cork. A thick wire protruded through the cork and into the water. The jar received a charge by bringing the exposed end of the wire into contact with an electrostatic **generator**. The modern equivalent of the Leyden jar is called a **capacitor** (condenser).

Electricity and Magnetism

is because the balloon's excess of negative electrons attracts the positive parts of atoms in the wall. The balloon will also attract strands of hair or bits of tissue paper in the same way.

Static charges usually discharge gradually into the air, especially on damp days. But sometimes, static can be shocking. For example, as you walk across a nylon or wool carpet on a cold, dry day, the contact between your shoes and the carpet causes static charge to build up in your body, especially if you shuffle your feet. If you touch a metal doorknob, the charge has somewhere to go, so it leaps across or discharges to the doorknob. You feel this as a tiny electric shock, and you may see it as a spark. The same discharge of static happens when your hair "crackles" as you take off a wool sweater.

Uses of static

Electrostatic charge is very useful in many machines. One such machine is the photocopier. The charge is caused by light shining onto a rotating drum that is coated with the metal selenium. The charged parts of the drum are in the pattern of the document to be copied. These charged parts attract tiny particles of the toner, or "ink." As the drum rolls past a sheet of paper, it transfers its toner to the paper. The toner is then heat-sealed onto the paper.

Attract or repel?

Opposite charges—that is, positive and negative charges—attract each other. But charges that are alike— positive and positive, or negative and negative—do not. They push away, or repel, each other.

Fine sprays, such as spray paint, work because of the way that like charges repel each other. The spray droplets pass an electrically charged surface that gives them their own charge. The droplets all have the same

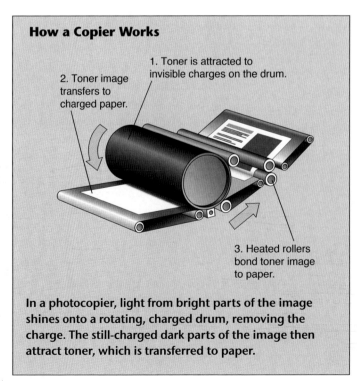

How a Copier Works

1. Toner is attracted to invisible charges on the drum.

2. Toner image transfers to charged paper.

3. Heated rollers bond toner image to paper.

In a photocopier, light from bright parts of the image shines onto a rotating, charged drum, removing the charge. The still-charged dark parts of the image then attract toner, which is transferred to paper.

Spray droplets and powders, as in this "crop-duster" plane, can all be given the same electrical charge. Then they push away from each other and spread out evenly, instead of sticking in clumps.

Measuring electric charge

An electroscope is an instrument that detects the presence of static electricity. It consists of two very thin leaves (strips) of metal foil dangling from a metal hook. When the hook is near a source of static electricity, some of the electrons in the hook are either pushed to the leaves or pulled from them, depending on whether the charge is positive or negative. Either way, the two leaves end up with the same charge, so they repel each other, bending apart like an upside-down "V." The stronger the charge, the farther apart the leaves move.

charge, so they push away from each other. This makes the droplets spread out, equally spaced, to give a smooth, even coat of paint. Some crop-dusting planes use a similar system to make the powdery particles spread out evenly. On the other hand, air filters use the attraction of opposite charges. They give floating particles of dust a charge, so that they stick to a metal grid that has the opposite charge.

An early version of the electroscope was used by the French scientist Charles de Coulomb (1736–1806) during the 1780s. The coulomb, a unit of measure describing the amount of charge of an object, is named for him.

ROBERT VAN DE GRAAFF: THE GENERATOR

U.S. engineer and physicist Robert van de Graaff (1901–1967) became associate professor of physics at the Massachusetts Institute of Technology (MIT) in Cambridge, Massachusetts, in 1934. In 1929, he devised a way of storing electrostatic charge on a hollow metal ball. This led to his invention of high-voltage static electricity machines for scientific research, which became known as van de Graaff generators. Van de Graaff left MIT in 1960 to set up a company making his machines. The designs are still used today for high-voltage physics. The biggest produce charges of many millions of volts.

A Pathway for Electricity

Substances and materials that easily carry an electric current are known as electrical conductors. Most metals are good conductors and are used in wires, cables, and electrical equipment. The arrangement of atoms inside a metal, and the number of electrons in each atom, mean the electrons can hop easily from one atom to the next, and cause a flow of current.

One of the best conductors is the metal silver. It is too expensive for ordinary electrical wires and cables, however, so these are usually made of copper. Copper wiring is far less expensive, does not rust, and is still a good conductor. Often special combinations of metals, known as **alloys**, are made for electrical equipment. Many overhead power lines (electricity cables) are alloys of the lightweight metal aluminum.

Insulators

The opposite of an electrical conductor is an electrical **insulator**. This hardly carries electricity at all. Good insulators include dry air, glass, plastics, wood, cardboard, paper, textiles, and ceramics such as pottery or porcelain.

Plastics are especially useful as insulators. Plastic can be made into many

shapes and lasts a long time. That is why electric wires have plastic coverings. It also explains why many electrical equipment pieces are inside plastic casings. The careful use of conductors and insulators means that we can safely channel and control electricity's flow.

Wires carrying very powerful electricity are held up on a stack of plate-like disks made from a very good insulating material. The material is usually some form of ceramic (clay-based) substance, such as the type used to make plates and cups.

SUPERCONDUCTORS

Substances known as **superconductors** have virtually no resistance at all to electric current. This is true, however, only when these substances are cooled to temperatures far below zero. Researchers are trying to develop a superconductor that will work at ordinary temperatures. This would help to save the huge amounts of electricity that are lost, mainly as heat, in long-distance power lines and other equipment.

Circuits

Two needs must be met for electricity to flow. One is a pushing force, such as a battery, to get the electrons moving. The other is a complete pathway for the current to flow around or to follow. This pathway is known as a **circuit**. A circuit is a route of conductors from one terminal (contact) of the battery to the other.

A Simple Circuit

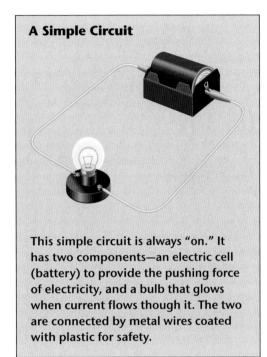

This simple circuit is always "on." It has two components—an electric cell (battery) to provide the pushing force of electricity, and a bulb that glows when current flows though it. The two are connected by metal wires coated with plastic for safety.

A typical flashlight has a simple circuit. One battery terminal connects by a metal wire or strip to one terminal of the bulb. The other bulb terminal has a wire or metal strip connected to the switch, and

UNITS OF ELECTRICITY

UNIT	MEANING	NAMED AFTER
Volt	Pushing force, or strength, of electricity	Italian scientist Alessandro Volta (1745–1827)
Amp	Amount of current flowing (number of electrons)	French scientist André-Marie Ampère (1775–1836)
Ohm	Resistance of a conductor	German scientist Georg Simon Ohm (1787–1854)

An On-Off Circuit

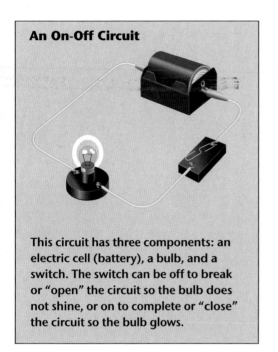

This circuit has three components: an electric cell (battery), a bulb, and a switch. The switch can be off to break or "open" the circuit so the bulb does not shine, or on to complete or "close" the circuit so the bulb glows.

then another wire or strip from the switch connected to the other battery terminal.

Switching on

When the flashlight is off, the circuit is not complete. The switch has a small gap between its contacts. The gap is filled with an insulator—air. Electricity cannot flow through the switch or around the circuit. Electrical engineers say the circuit is "broken." This does not mean it is damaged—it means the circuit is incomplete.

Switch on the flashlight, and the contacts inside the switch come together. The circuit is now complete, and electricity flows. The current passes through the thin, coiled wire inside the bulb, called the filament. The current has to push hard to get through the filament, and this makes heat. In fact, the filament gets so hot that it glows with a bright white light and the bulb shines.

The bulb filament itself conducts electricity, but does so poorly, which causes it to shine. The filament pushes against or resists the flow of current. It is said to have a high resistance, compared to a copper or silver wire, which has very little resistance. Engineers make wires and other conductors with different amounts of electrical resistance, for various purposes.

Electric cells

How do the electrons start moving? In a flashlight, the push comes from batteries or electric cells. Technically, a battery is several electric cells joined together.

TWITCHING LEGS

Italian scientist Luigi Galvani (1737–1798) thought he had discovered "animal electricity." While cutting up a dead frog, its leg muscles twitched. Galvani had unknowingly made a simple battery from his metal knife, metal cutting frame, and a salt solution that kept the frog's muscles damp. The electricity flowed through the muscles and caused the leg to "kick."

A flashlight with two or three "batteries" has two or three electric cells, and, together, they make one battery. In daily life, however, the word battery is often used to describe one electric cell.

Parts of an electric cell

A typical battery (or cell) contains a mixture of various chemicals. It changes the energy contained inside the chemicals into electrical energy. A battery generally includes four parts:

- A casing
- A positive terminal or electrode, called an **anode**
- A negative terminal or electrode, called the **cathode**. Sometimes, this is the same as the casing.
- A substance between the positive and negative electrodes, which is the **electrolyte**

Inside the battery, when the circuit is complete, the tiny particles of chemicals react with each other. The electrolyte "steals" negative electrons from the positive terminal. Meanwhile, it gives electrons to the negative terminal. These electrons are pushed, or repelled, from the negative

terminal, pass around the circuit, and are attracted back to the positive terminal. We often think of electricity as "flowing" from positive to negative. But the electrons themselves travel the opposite way.

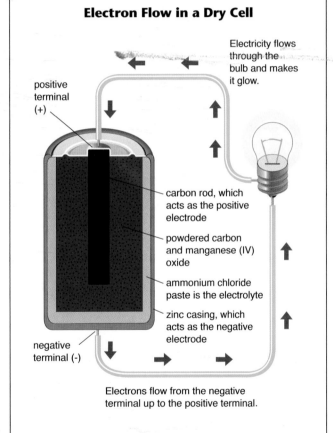

Electron Flow in a Dry Cell

Electricity flows through the bulb and makes it glow.

positive terminal (+)

carbon rod, which acts as the positive electrode

powdered carbon and manganese (IV) oxide

ammonium chloride paste is the electrolyte

zinc casing, which acts as the negative electrode

negative terminal (-)

Electrons flow from the negative terminal up to the positive terminal.

A traditional "dry cell" has a zinc canister that acts as both the casing and negative terminal. A carbon rod protected by powder acts as the positive terminal, and a paste of ammonium chloride acts as the electrolyte between the two.

ALESSANDRO VOLTA: THE FIRST BATTERY

Italian nobleman Alessandro Volta (1745–1827) was a professor at two universities—in Como and Pavia, Italy. After Luigi Galvani's frog muscle experiments, Volta tested various metals and chemicals to see if they made electricity. His invention of 1799–1800 was a "tower" of alternating zinc and copper disks with layers of saltwater-soaked cardboard between them. His experiment was the first electrical battery, or cell, giving a source of steady electric current. It became known as the voltaic pile and allowed a range of new electrical experiments.

The first electricity-making battery, made by Alessandro Volta, had a stack of metal and saltwater-soaked cardboard disks. It produced only one to two volts—about the same as a modern flashlight battery.

AN AMAZING INVENTION

"A battery of an immense capacity; but which further infinitely surpasses the power of those batteries [Leyden jars] in that it does not need, as they do, to be charged in advance by means of an outside source. . . it can give the disturbance every time that it is properly touched, no matter how often."

Alessandro Volta (1745–1827),
Italian nobleman and scientist.

Types of batteries

There are dozens of battery or cell types. Dry cells, like those in flashlights and toys, have a gel or powder inside. The particular chemical gives the battery its name, such as alkaline or lithium. Wet cells have a liquid electrolyte. The large battery in a car or truck is an example of this type. Its electrolyte is very strong sulfuric acid, and its electrodes are made of the heavy metal lead. This type of battery is sometimes known as a lead-acid accumulator.

Primary and secondary

A **primary cell**, or battery, gradually uses all of its chemical energy. Eventually, it can no longer produce electricity and is discharged (or dead) and useless. A **secondary cell** can be recharged, which means putting electricity into it to make the chemicals change back into their original form. Rechargeable batteries—secondary cells— are found in many pieces of electrical equipment, such as mobile phones. Some are known as "nicads" because they contain the metals nickel and cadmium. A vehicle battery also functions as a secondary cell. It is continually recharged by energy from the engine. That's why you can "jump" a dead battery to start a car.

Types of circuits

The way that parts, or components, are linked in a circuit is important. If the components are connected in a linear fashion, first one, then the next, and so on, this is a **series circuit**. An example is a battery connected by a wire to a bulb, then

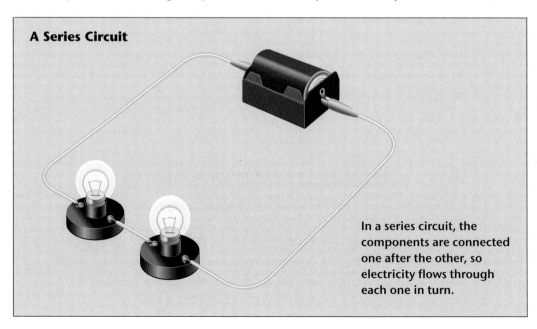

A Series Circuit

In a series circuit, the components are connected one after the other, so electricity flows through each one in turn.

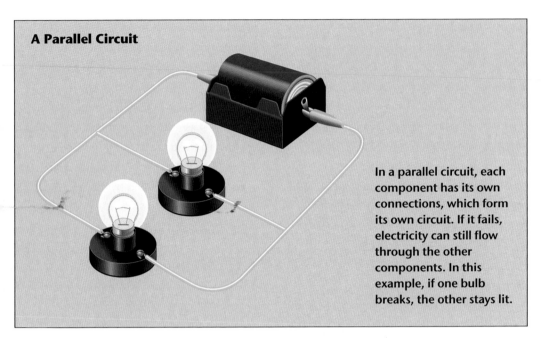

A Parallel Circuit

In a parallel circuit, each component has its own connections, which form its own circuit. If it fails, electricity can still flow through the other components. In this example, if one bulb breaks, the other stays lit.

another wire to another bulb, and back to the battery. The same amount of electricity flows through each bulb. But the added resistance of both bulbs means the flow is weaker and the bulbs shine less brightly. Also, if one bulb fails, the circuit is broken and the other bulb goes out. Some Christmas tree light sets are "series" lights—either they all light up or none do. The trick is finding the burned-out bulb.

Parallel circuits

Another design is the **parallel circuit**. Here, each component has its own circuit so the same amount of electricity flows through each. An example is a battery connected by two wires to two lightbulbs, and then two more wires back to the battery. The full amount of electricity flows through both bulbs, so they shine brightly. If one bulb fails, the other still shines. But

ELECTRICITY FROM CRYSTALS

When certain kinds of crystals are compressed or stretched, they produce tiny amounts of electricity. This is called the **piezoelectric effect**. The reverse happens, too—an electric current passing through a crystal causes it to change shape. A crystal commonly used for this effect is quartz (silicon dioxide, often found in sand grains). A fast-changing electric current can make a quartz crystal vibrate an exact number of times each second, so this combination of electricity and crystals is often used for quartz watches.

LEMON BATTERY

You can make a battery by pushing objects made of two different metals into a lemon. The metals are the electrodes of the cell. The lemon juice is the electrolyte. If you connect a lightbulb to the circuit, it will shine weakly.

the electricity is being used twice as fast as in the series circuit, so the battery in a parallel circuit runs out in half the time. Most household wiring is parallel, so that if one lightbulb fails, the others stay lit.

ELECTROPLATING

Electroplating is a method of coating an object with a thin layer of metal. It uses an electric current to make the coating stick. Electroplating is used to make metals more durable, such as steel food cans or car parts coated with rust-resistant zinc. It also can be used to enhance the look of a metal object, such as silver plating cutlery or gold plating jewelry.

In electroplating, the coating substance is dissolved in a solution. Its **molecules** (groups of atoms) split into positive and negative parts called **ions.** The electric current moves the ions. Positive ions, such as those in the precious metals gold and silver, are attracted to the object to be plated, which has a negative electric charge.

Plastic sheets are coated with copper by electroplating. Next, some of the copper will be removed to leave strips that will connect many electrical components on a circuit board.

Mysterious Magnetism

In ancient times, people noticed that certain rocks, such as lodestone (magnetite), had interesting qualities. Two pieces of magnetite could pull or push against each other and could pull items that contained iron—as if grabbed by an invisible hand. Scientists now know much more about magnetism, yet mysteries remain.

Q&A

WHY THE NAME *MAGNET*?

Magnetism may be named after a region in Turkey called Magnesia. The natural magnetic rock now known as magnetite, or lodestone, was common there, and lumps of the rock could be picked up and tested for their invisible force.

Like its "twin partner" electricity, magnetism is based on atoms and their electrons. As described earlier, electrons have a negative charge. They whirl around the atom's nucleus, like planets around the Sun. At the same time, each electron spins around, as Earth does while orbiting the Sun. The electron's combined movements of spinning around itself and also orbiting the nucleus combine to produce a tiny force of magnetism within each atom.

All lined up

In most substances, the magnetic forces of the electrons are arranged at random and point in different directions. There is no overall magnetism. In a magnet, all these tiny magnet forces point the same way. They add up to produce tiny areas of magnetism, called **domains** (see below), which, in turn, combine to form the whole magnet.

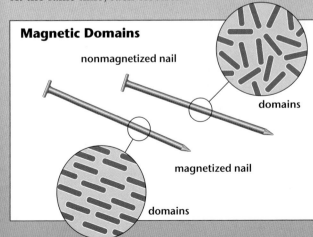

Magnetic Domains

nonmagnetized nail

domains

magnetized nail

domains

In the nonmagnetized nail, the magnetic domains are jumbled up. Their "north" and "south" **poles** cancel each other out. In the magnetized nail, the domains have been aligned in the same direction. The nail now has a "north" and "south" pole.

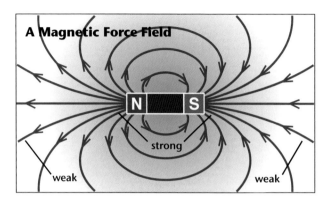

A Magnetic Force Field

N S

strong

weak weak

A bar magnet's field is usually shown by imaginary lines of force. The farther away from the magnet, the weaker the magnetism. The strongest magnetism is where the lines are closest, at the ends, or poles, of the magnet.

Iron has the best arrangement of atoms and electrons for forming domains. For this reason, most magnets are made of iron. A few other metals show similar properties, including nickel, cobalt, gadolinium,

neodymium, and dysprosium. Other metals are not magnetic, which means they cannot be made into a magnet and are not attracted by one. Most soft drink cans are made of aluminum, which is not magnetic. A food can consists mainly of steel, which contains iron, and is magnetic.

Magnetic field

The force around a magnet is called its **magnetic field**. This field is usually imagined as invisible lines of magnetic force. The lines of force get weaker as we move farther from the magnet. The lines come together to make powerful magnetism at two places: the magnet's poles. These are the north (positive) pole and the south (negative) pole.

POWER OF MAGNETS

The strength of a magnetic field can be measured in teslas. This unit of measurement—named for the scientist Nikola Tesla (1856–1943)—reflects the number of lines of magnetic force in the field. (See biography box on Nikola Tesla, page 35.)

MAGNETIC FIELD	STRENGTH IN TESLAS
Earth's magnetic field at the equator	0.00005
Small magnet in earphones	0.001
Refrigerator magnet	0.05
Big loudspeaker magnet	0.5
Medical magnetic resonance imaging (MRI) scanner	1–7
Scientific research equipment	50+

Electricity and Magnetism

Opposites attract; likes repel

The main principle of magnetism is that opposite poles attract and like poles repel. This means a north pole of one magnet pulls the south pole of another. But two north poles, or two south poles, push away from each other. This is similar to electrostatic charges, where positive attracts negative, but two positives or two negatives repel.

Magnets can be made in any number of shapes. Bars or "U" shapes (horseshoes) have poles at the ends. Disk or button magnets have poles on either side. There are also ring, tube, and ball magnets. But a magnet's magnetism does not last forever. It fades over time. It can also be destroyed by hammering or heating, which jumbles up the tiny domains.

Magnetic Earth

Planet Earth has a center, or core, composed of iron and nickel. The inner part of the core is solid, but the outer part of the core is liquid. Currents set into motion by temperature differences in the molten (melted) rock cause this part of the core to swirl slowly, like thick molasses. Scientists think that this movement, combined with the effects of the planet's rotation, generate a magnetic field that causes the entire Earth to act like a giant magnet. Its magnetic north and south poles are near, but not at, the geographic North and South poles. (The geographic poles are the places around which Earth turns once each day.)

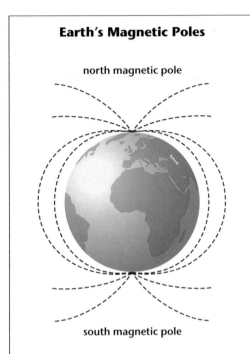

Earth's Magnetic Poles

north magnetic pole

south magnetic pole

Earth is like a giant magnet, with invisible lines of magnetic force extending up and around, through the air, and even into space. The lines come together at the north and south magnetic poles.

A magnetic compass is usually a round casing containing a small needlelike magnet that is free to move. It usually swings around to point north-south. This is because the magnetic compass's poles are attracted to the unlike poles of Earth. The first magnetic compasses were slivers of lodestone, used in China almost two thousand years ago. Since then, they have been improved and used by sailors, explorers, mapmakers, and travelers to find their way.

WILLIAM GILBERT

William Gilbert (1544–1603) was a British scientist who studied magnets. His main career was in medicine. He was president of the Royal College of Physicians and attended Queen Elizabeth I and King James I. Gilbert also carried out many studies on magnets and electricity, suggested that Earth was a giant magnet, and introduced the term *magnetic pole*. His book, *De Magnete*, was seventeen years' worth of experiment results. The book captured his thinking on magnets—as well as all the trustworthy information on magnets at the time. In it, Gilbert included a description of how to turn an iron bar into a magnet by rubbing it with another magnet.

There are hundreds of modern uses for magnets. They include note-holders on refrigerators, cupboard door catches, knife-blade holders, and removable magnetic signs stuck to vehicles. Some credit cards and security cards have a strip with a tiny series of magnetic patterns. These strips give the card's code number when run through a magnetic reader (the machine through which a credit card is swiped).

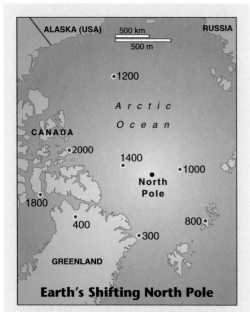

Earth's Shifting North Pole

Scientific estimates show that the magnetic north pole (red dots) has moved many thousands of miles between the years 300 and 2000. In 2005, it was in the Canadian Arctic, more than 560 miles (900 kilometers) from the geographic North Pole. Now it is heading for Siberia, Russia, and picking up speed by shifting 25 miles (40 kilometers) per year.

MAGNETS AND THE EARTH

"[Iron and magnets] retain the first faculties in nature, the faculties of attracting each other, of moving, and of adjusting by the position of the world and the terrestrial globe."

William Gilbert, (1544–1603), English doctor and scientist.

CHAPTER 5

Electricity and Magnetism

Magnets are not the only objects with magnetic fields around them. Any material conducting electricity makes a magnetic field around itself. This includes everything from the thin wires of earphones to the giant power lines reaching across the countryside. This happens because an electric current is electrons on the move, all in the same direction inside the conductor, which is similar to the way electrons spin and align in a magnet.

The creation of a magnetic field around a conductor is known as the electromagnetic effect. The magnetism is exactly the same as around an ordinary magnet. It has poles and lines of force, and it gets weaker with distance. The only difference is that when the current stops, so does the magnetism. When it is switched on again, the magnetism reappears.

How a Solenoid Works

invisible lines of magnetic force

north pole

south pole

coils of solenoid

battery

wire

A solenoid is a coil of wire carrying an electric current. It makes a magnetic field around itself by the electromagnetic effect.

Magnetism from electricity

The magnetic field around an ordinary wire carrying electricity is much too weak for us to notice. If the current-carrying wire is made into a coil, however, the individual magnetic fields of the coil's turns combine to form a single stronger magnetic field. The tube-shaped coil of wire is known as a **solenoid**.

A current flowing through the solenoid can pull an iron bar into the middle of the coil. Lots of switches and locks contain this type of solenoid mechanism. When you operate a vehicle's remote-controlled central locking system,

At a scrap yard, a powerful electromagnet attracts iron-containing, or ferrous, metals (such as food cans), lifts and moves them, and then drops them when the electricity is switched off.

for example, the current flows through a solenoid in each door lock. This current pulls an iron bar attached to the lock mechanism, which slides along to lock or unlock the door.

Electromagnets

With an iron bar inside the coil, the magnetic field is concentrated even more. The iron bar becomes a bar magnet. The magnetism of this bar magnet can be switched on and off by switching the electric current through the solenoid on and off. This device is known as an **electromagnet**. Ordinary magnets that are magnetic all the time (with no need

for an electric current) are often called permanent magnets to distinguish them from electromagnets.

Big electromagnets are used in scrapyards to lift and sort metals for recycling. They attract only iron-containing, or ferrous, metals, and leave nonferrous metals, such as aluminum, behind. These magnets can even lift heavy objects containing iron, such as steel container drums and cars.

The electric motor

Like ordinary magnets, electromagnets obey the rule that like poles repel and unlike poles attract. This is the basis of one

MICHAEL FARADAY AND JOSEPH HENRY: SUPREME INVESTIGATORS

Two great scientists carried out early experiments on electricity and magnetism at about the same time. They were Michael Faraday (1791–1867) in England and Joseph Henry (1797–1878) in the United States. Faraday, called the greatest researcher of his age, was also an outstanding teacher. He started as a bookbinder but was fascinated by science. He took a job as an assistant to Humphry Davy, head of London's Royal Institution. Faraday would later have this job. He began his long career in chemistry, but he switched to electricity and magnetism in 1830. He determined the principles of **electrolysis**, discovered **electromagnetic induction**, and invented basic types of electric motors, generators, and **transformers**.

Henry wanted to be a writer and actor, but found he was better at science. In 1832, he became a teacher at the College of New Jersey (later known as Princeton). There, he worked on improving the design of the electromagnet so it could lift more than one ton (one tonne). Henry discovered electromagnetic induction before Faraday, but he did not publish his reports until after Faraday. In 1846, Henry became the first director of the Smithsonian Institution. He was still busy conducting research at the age of eighty.

of the most useful machines in the modern world: the electric motor. A basic motor consists of a coil of wire, like a solenoid, but on a long rod or shaft that is able to spin around. This coil is the **armature**. Two poles of a permanent magnet are on either side of the coil.

AN OPEN MIND

"Seeds of great discoveries are constantly floating around us, but they only take root in minds well prepared to receive them."

Joseph Henry (1797–1878),
U.S. scientist, engineer and inventor.

SUCCESSFUL FAILURES

"The failures are just as important as the successes."

Michael Faraday (1791–1867),
English scientist and researcher,
on the importance of all
experimental results.

When the electricity switches on, the armature becomes an electromagnet with its own poles. If the electromagnet's north pole is near the permanent magnet's north pole, these two repel. The armature's north pole is attracted to the permanent magnet's south pole on the other side. This makes the armature spin around for half a turn. A switching device on the shaft, called the **commutator**, consists of a metal collar divided into two halves, with each collar joined to one end of the armature wire. Two wire contacts called **brushes** press on either side of the commutator and feed electricity to it and to the armature.

Reversing the current

As the armature spins half a turn, the commutator contacts move around half a turn, so that in effect, they exchange brushes. This reverses the electric current, which reverses the armature's magnetic poles. Its north becomes south, and now repels the nearby south pole of the permanent magnet. The same push-pull forces happen again, making the armature spin further—and the commutator reverses the current again. The armature keeps spinning as the commutator keeps switching the current. This causes the electric motor to turn around, changing electrical energy into kinetic (movement) energy.

High-speed "**bullet trains,**" like the Japanese *Shinkansen*, receive electricity from overhead wires to power electric motors next to their wheels. They can travel faster than 155 miles (250 km) per hour.

HANS CHRISTIAN ØRSTED: FINDING THE CONNECTION

Danish scientist Hans Christian Ørsted (1777–1851) studied physics and pharmacology (drugs and medications). In 1806, after traveling as a journalist and a public speaker, he became professor of physics at the University of Copenhagen, Denmark. In 1820, while showing experiments to students, he held a magnetic compass near a wire carrying electricity—and saw that the compass needle moved. He suspected the wire had a magnetic field around it, and he went on to show this was true. Ørsted's discovery proved a basic connection between electricity and magnetism and led to a burst of research among other scientists. The physical unit for the strength of a magnetic field is named after him.

Ørsted also worked on compression (squeezing) of gases and liquids, and discovered the substance piperine, which gives pepper its spicy flavor.

MOTOR FACTS

- The fastest motor in an electric shaver turns at 13,000 revolutions per minute (rpm)—which is more than 200 times each second.

- The wheel motors on some electric trains weigh more than 5.6 tons (5 tonnes) each.

- The smallest motors are rotor nanomotors, which are so tiny that 1,000 in a row would stretch just .04 inch (1 mm). They are being developed for tiny robots that could one day be put into a human body, for example, to remove troublesome blockages in blood vessels.

Motors galore

Electric motors come in thousands of sizes and shapes. Each motor has its own features, such as a fast-turning speed or a slow but strong rotation. Most have several sets of coils on the armature, connected to several segments of the commutator. This arrangement gives a smoother, more regular turning force.

Tiny motors the size of rice grains are built into certain types of microscopic medical equipment. Giant motors the size of cars can be found in factory equipment.

There are dozens of electric motors in the typical house. You will find them in CD/DVD players, computer drives, hair dryers, food blenders, fans, air

THE "HAND RULES"

The left-hand and right-hand rules are easy ways to remember the relationships between magnetic field, current, and movement. The finger positions for either hand are the same: index pointed forward, thumb pointed up, middle finger pointed to side.

In the left-hand rule, if the forefinger points along the magnetic field and the middle finger points along the direction of the current, the thumb shows the direction in which the motor will turn (rotate).

In the right-hand rule (shown right), again the forefinger points toward the magnetic field flow, and the thumb indicates the direction in which the motor moves. The middle finger indicates the direction of the current flow produced in the coils of the motor.

Electrical engineers use the the left- and right-hand rules to predict the direction of movement, magnetic field, or current. They (and we) can apply these rules to equipment such as electromagnets, electric motors, and generators.

conditioners and heaters, washing machines and dryers, refrigerators and freezers, microwave ovens, and even battery-operated toys such as cars, boats, and planes.

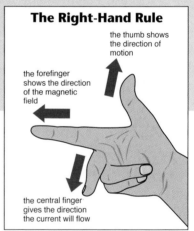

The Right-Hand Rule

the thumb shows the direction of motion

the forefinger shows the direction of the magnetic field

the central finger gives the direction the current will flow

ENERGY EFFICIENT

The electric motor is one of the best ways to change one form of energy—in this case, electricity—into motion. Car engines convert only about one third of their fuel energy into movement.

MOTOR OR ENGINE	% OF ENERGY TURNED INTO MOVEMENT
electric motor	more than 90
steam turbine	60
gas turbine	55
diesel engine	40
gasoline engine	35
steam engine	10

CHAPTER 6

Generators and Grids

We use electricity every day, but where does it come from? In portable items, such as mobile phones, it comes from batteries or electric cells. The second main type of supply is much more powerful. All over the country, electric power plants are connected by a system known as **power grids**. The United States has more than six thousand of these plants. The electricity they produce moves around the country along nearly half a million miles (nearly 800,000 km) of high-voltage transmission lines. This movement is directed by more than one hundred control centers that monitor the distribution of power and direct the energy to where it is needed most. As you will see, high-voltage electricity goes through a series of changes before it reaches your home and is ready for you to use.

A Power Grid

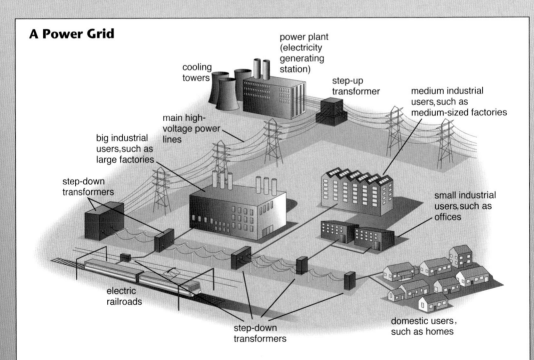

Electricity from the power plant is "stepped up" in voltage for long-distance transportation and stepped down in stages for different kinds of use, from industries and offices to houses and stores.

Generating electricity by burning coal, oil, and gas uses up vast amounts of natural resources. It also gives off wasted heat from huge cooling towers, as well as **greenhouse gases** that cause global warming.

NIKOLA TESLA

Croatian-born U.S. scientist Nikola Tesla (1856–1943) made great advances in electricity generation, transformers, and motors. He saw that alternating current was a better power supply than direct current, although his former employer, Thomas Edison, disagreed. In 1888, Tesla devised the induction motor, which has no commutator or brushes. This motor is widely used today in home appliances such as vacuum cleaners and washing machines. Tesla joined Edison's rival, George Westinghouse, to develop and manufacture his many inventions, including a type of fluorescent light. He also invented the high-voltage Tesla coil, which can make sparks 130 feet (40 meters) long!

DC and AC

The electric current from batteries and cells flows steadily in one direction only, like water in a river. This is known as direct current, or DC. The electricity that comes to us through our wall outlets is much stronger than a battery's DC. It also changes, or alternates, its direction of flow many times each second. This is known as alternating current, or AC. In the United States, the electric current does this 60 times each second. This is written as 60 Hz (Hertz).

Why an AC grid?

There are several reasons that AC is used. First, sending AC long distances through power lines wastes less energy compared to DC. Second, generators at power plants produce AC more efficiently than they produce DC. Third, AC voltage

THOMAS EDISON: ELECTRICITY TO PEOPLE

U.S. inventor Thomas Edison (1847–1931) went to school for about three months when he was seven years old. After that, his mother taught him at home. But Edison's curiosity and genius for gadgets led to thousands of inventions over his lifetime. He invented such things as a type of microphone, the phonograph (an early sound recorder-player), the electric lightbulb, and a moving picture machine. Edison set up the world's first large-scale electricity generators at Pearl Street, New York City, in 1882, to supply the Wall Street district. When he died, millions of people around the world turned off their electric lights for a short time in his memory.

electricity involves keeping the magnet stable but making it stronger.

Generators

A basic electric generator (sometimes called a dynamo) changes mechanical motion into electricity through electromagnetic induction, as described above. A simple design for a generator resembles an electric motor—a coil of wire spins around a magnet. A wire keeps passing through the lines of magnetic force, making a current flow in the wire. Movement, or kinetic energy, is converted to the type of electrical energy called DC.

In a power plant, generators have two massive sets of coils. One is the rotor, which spins on a shaft. The other is a stator, which is like a tube around the rotor. It

and current can be "transformed," while DC cannot.

In a power plant (electricity generating plant), a generator uses the opposite process to electromagnetism. This is converting magnetism to electricity, which is known as electromagnetic induction. It happens when a conductor, such as a wire, and a magnetic field move past each other. Imagine the wire passing through the magnet's lines of force. When this happens, electricity flows in the wire. If the movement of the magnet stops, so does the electricity. Another way to generate

THE TROUBLE WITH EDISON

"If Edison had a needle to find in a haystack, he would proceed at once with the diligence of the bee to examine straw after straw. . . knowing that a little theory and calculation would have saved him ninety percent of his labor."

Nikola Tesla (1856–1943), Croatian-born U.S. scientist, who often argued with Edison.

THE ELECTRIC GUITAR

The electric guitar works by electromagnetic induction. Its metal strings vibrate in the field of a powerful bar magnet in the guitar's pickup, mounted just below the strings. The pickup is a device for changing vibrations into electrical signals in the wire coil around the magnet. The signals are fed into an amplifier and speakers.

stays still. Electric current is fed into one coil set, usually the rotor, which becomes an electromagnet. As it spins, its magnetic force fields pass through the coils of the stator to produce electricity, which flows into the grid. The initial electrical energy of the rotor is increased and added to the kinetic (movement) energy that spins the rotor, which generates greater electrical energy going out of the stator.

Spinning magnetism

There are several sets of coils in the rotor and stator. As a rotor coil's magnetic field approaches a stator coil, it induces (causes) electricity to

flow one way. As the rotor coil spins past and away, the stator current flows the other way. This happens many times each second. It means the electricity changes direction very fast and enters the power grid as alternating current, AC.

Energy changes

A power plant is part of a sequence, or chain, of energy changes. For example, in a coal-fired power plant, coal burns and converts its chemical energy to heat energy. This boils water into steam that blasts past the fan-like blades of a turbine to make kinetic energy. The turbine is connected to the generator and spins its shaft to change kinetic energy to electrical energy.

There are many sources of energy for different types of generators: coal, gas, oil,

An engineer in the control room of an electric power plant monitors the generators and keeps track of how much electricity is produced.

CONSERVING ELECTRICITY—A GOOD CHOICE!

When we conserve electricity, we help reduce the use of many kinds of energy resources. We also help reduce pollution, conserve **fossil fuels**, and lower the amounts of greenhouse gases causing global warming. Even simple actions—such as turning off lights, televisions, and heaters in unused rooms—can help.

nuclear, biofuels (plant material or animal waste), geothermal heat from the Earth, flowing water (hydropower), blowing wind, sunlight, the rise and fall of tides, and wave action.

Transforming electricity

As mentioned before, another advantage of AC is that its voltage (strength) and current (quantity of flow), can be changed by a **transformer**. This machine has sets of coils that "transform," or alter, the high voltages used for transporting the electricity into the lower voltages useable by homes and industries. Transformers do change the energy by increasing, or "stepping up," the voltage for transportation, and decreasing, or "stepping down," the high voltages for use. Transformers, however, do not produce extra electricity from nothing. As the voltage increases, the current (quantity) in

Overhead wires, or power lines, carry electricity with a strength of half a million volts or more. The wires take the electricity long distances from power plants to cities.

Did You Know

IGNITION COIL
A typical car battery is 12 volts. A type of transformer called an ignition coil in the car increases this to bursts of 20,000-plus volts for the spark plugs, which ignite the gasoline vapors in the engine.

amps decreases. The total amount of electrical energy stays the same.

Electricity produced by the generator at a power plant is usually about 25,000 volts. A transformer steps up its voltage to as many as 500,000 volts. Besides being more efficient, the higher voltage is necessary to push the electricity long distances. The electricity then moves out into the power grid and travels along high-voltage transmission lines.

Electricity to the home

When electricity reaches the electrical substation nearest to where you live, the voltage is stepped down so that it can be sent along smaller lines called distribution lines to your neighborhood. There, smaller transformers—often at the top of power poles—step down the voltage to a safe level

ELECTRICITY SOURCES

Around the world, people generate electricity from many energy sources. Even cow manure or chicken droppings can be burned in power plants. Overall, our global electricity comes from these sources:

Coal	38%
Hydro (water power)	20%
Nuclear	15%
Gas	15%
Oil	10%
Other (wind, solar, tidal, etc.)	2%

to use in your home. The electricity follows a line leading directly to the meter that measures how much electricity your family uses. From there, it goes to a service panel, where circuit breakers or fuses protect the wiring in your home from getting overloaded.

Fuel cells use water (H_2O) to generate electricity. They produce no greenhouse gases or other fumes. Fuel cells are being tested in many places, such as this electric bus in London, England.

Electronics

Modern life includes electrical machines and gadgets, from bullet trains to cooling fans. We also use electronic items and equipment, from the Internet and supercomputers to games, cell phones, and MP3 players.

What's the difference between electric and electronic? Both use flows of electrons as electric currents. In general, an electrical device has moving parts like solenoids, motors, and switches. Electronic devices lack obvious moving parts. They control and manipulate currents at the level of atoms and electrons, using the direct effects of electricity and magnetism—electricity controlling itself.

Electronic circuits

Some electronic circuits are contained in little plastic blocks. They are known as integrated circuits (ICs) because the electronic components are connected, or integrated, as the circuit is made. ICs are also called microchips. These components are microscopic, with thousands fitting into a circuit as small as this "o." They are manufactured on a slim wafer or "chip."

The electronic chip is usually made of a **semiconductor**, such as silicon. Semiconductors can work as either conductors or insulators. Their function depends on conditions, such as a nearby electric current or magnetic field, a pattern

The protective plastic "black box" in the middle of this circuit board contains a microchip. Small metal strips or "legs" along each side connect it to the other board components.

of incoming signals, or varying temperatures. Changing the conditions, such as adding a tiny pulse of electricity, alters the flow of electrons.

Microchips

Many electronic circuits contain microversions of larger electrical components. These components might include resistors to reduce current flow and capacitors to store electric charge.

TUBES AND TRANSISTORS

- One of the earliest electronic devices was the tube (thermionic tube), with a beam of electrons given off by a very hot metal plate into the vacuum within a glass tube.
- In 1904, English scientist Ambrose Fleming (1849–1945) made an early model of a tube, the diode.
- U.S. physicist Lee de Forest (1873–1961) devised the triode tube, which worked as an amplifier, in 1906.
- In 1947, a team led by U.S. electronics engineer William Shockley (1910–1989) invented the transistor.
- The transistor did a similar job to the tube, but it was much smaller and lighter, more reliable, and used much less electricity.
- Transistors revolutionized electronics. One of their first applications was the portable "transistor radio."

Cell phones use low-power radio waves to carry their signals. Radio waves are part of the range, or spectrum, of combined electrical and magnetic energy—the **electromagnetic spectrum**.

Transistors are key components, and there are many kinds. Some use a small electric current to control a larger one, so they work as amplifiers. Others switch on different parts of their circuits according to the electronic signals fed to them.

Modern microchips have complex circuits usually designed with the help of computers. The components are made directly on the chip by methods such as etching. In acid etching, a strong chemical eats into different parts of the chip to shape the components. In laser etching, a laser beam burns the components into the chip.

WILLIAM SHOCKLEY

London-born U.S. electronics engineer William Shockley (1910–1989) led the team that invented the transistor in 1947. Their invention was the first "solid state" electrical component—that is, it had no moving parts. He worked mainly at Bell Laboratories in Murray Hill, New Jersey, with John Bardeen and Walter Brattain. They used crystals of germanium to control and amplify electrical currents, ushering in the "transistor age" of the 1950s. In 1956, the three scientists shared the Nobel Prize in physics. Shockley's insights and theories led to the development of the technology that is the foundation of modern electronics. Despite his great achievements, Shockley held racist views. Because of this, he died in disgrace.

(*From left to right*) Bardeen, Shockley, and Brattain invented the first transistor. This device made electrical equipment much smaller, lighter, and more reliable—and used less electrical energy.

Q&A WHAT IS THE ELECTROMAGNETIC SPECTRUM?

Electromagnetism (combined electricity and magnetism) forms waves and rays that travel through space at the speed of light. In fact, some of them are visible light. This range of waves is the electromagnetic spectrum, and we use every part of it in many ways, from communicating with space probes to cooking.

- The longest waves, with each wave stretching many miles, are radio waves for radio and TV.
- Next are microwaves, which extend from less than one inch (2.54 centimeters) to about 12 inches (30 cm) long.
- Increasingly shorter are infrared (heat rays), visible light rays, ultraviolet rays, and X-rays.
- Shortest are gamma rays, which are measured in microns (1 micron = 0.00004 inch).

Analog and digital

In analog technology, an electric current carries information by varying the voltage. Digital technology carries information in a series of "on" and "off" pulses of electricity. These pulses are often written as a series of 1s and 0s, with 1 for a pulse and 0 for a gap.

Digital electronics can send information in incredibly fast streams of on-off pulses. Digital information is much faster and more reliable than the analog style. Computers use digital technology.

There are thousands of types of electronic microchips. A computer, for example, includes memory chips, clock chips, and the central processing unit (microprocessor, or CPU). The memory chips store information. The clock chips control the timing of signals. The CPU receives and acts on instructions.

The future

Electronic devices such as microchips crop up in appliances, machines, and gadgets, the sizes of which constantly decrease even as the speed and performance of these devices increase. There may be a limit to how small and fast electronic devices can become, but designers keep improving the technology. Electrical engineers also strive to produce better electric cars, drills, blenders, and many other machines. Our reliance on electricity and electronics will continue to increase in the future.

The electromagnetic spectrum

In the electromagnetic spectrum, the waves are combined electrical and magnetic energy. A single "long wave" radio wave can be several miles (km) in length, while the lengths of microwaves are measured in a few inches, and each light wave is less than 1/25,000th of an inch (a thousandth of a mm) long.

GLOSSARY

alloy special combinations of metals that are often made for electrical equipment

amber fossilized tree resin. Our word *electricity* comes from the Greek word for amber, *elektron*.

amps (amperes) unit measuring the quantity, or amount, of electricity that flows

armature a coil of wire which can spin around on an axle or shaft

anode a positive terminal or electrode. In a Galvanic cell, the terminal charge is negative.

atoms the smallest particles of a substance

brushes blocklike contacts that feed electricity to the commutator on the shaft of an electric motor

bullet train high-speed electric train

capacitor device that stores electricity, usually as static charge

cathode a negative terminal or electrode (in a Galvanic cell, it is positive). Sometimes, this component is the electric cell's casing.

cell a device that produces electricity by chemical change. A dry cell has a gel or powder as the electrolyte. A wet cell has a liquid electrolyte.

circuit a pathway or route along which electricity flows

commutator a collarlike ring with two or more sections on the shaft of an electric motor, which feeds electricity to the rotating coils

conductor a material, such as metal, that carries electric current well

discharge in electricity, the sudden rush of electricity from one place to another, as in a spark or shock

domains tiny areas of magnetism

electrode a piece of metal that collects or releases electrons in an electric circuit

electrolysis chemical change in an electrolyte caused by an electric current flowing through it

electrolyte a substance that conducts electricity when molten or in solution

electromagnet a device that changes electrical energy into magnetism

electromagnetic pertaining to a magnetic force that has been created by electricity. For example, electricity flowing through a wire produces a magnetic field around the wire.

electromagnetic induction the result of magnetism (as a moving or changing magnetic field) producing a flow of electricity in a nearby wire

electromagnetic spectrum the complete range of electromagnetic radiation—gamma rays, X-rays, untraviolet radiation, visible light, infreared radiation, microwaves, and radio waves

electrons tiny particles with negative charge that go around or orbit the nucleus (central part) of an atom

fossil fuels fuels made by the process of fossilization millions of years ago, including oil, coal, and gas, which we burn for heat

generator a machine that makes electricity from movement energy

greenhouse gases gases, such as carbon dioxide, believed to contribute to the warming of Earth

insulator a material that carries electric current very badly or not at all

ion a chargd atom

magnetic field area around a magnet where its force of magnetism is effective

molecule a group of atoms

nervous system network of nerves inside an animal that carries information as tiny electrical nerve signals

neutrons tiny particles with neither positive nor negative charge, that is, neutral, found in the nucleus (central part) of an atom

nucleus the central or middle part of an atom, consisting of particles called protons and neutrons, and around which electrons orbit

ohm a unit of electrical resistance

parallel circuit an electric circuit in which the components are connected side by side, so current flows through them all at the same time

piezoelectric effect the production of electricity by applying stress to certain crystals.

poles the opposite ends of a magnet

power grid a system that connects electrical power plants

primary cell an electrical cell or battery that cannot be recharged and is useless when its chemical energy is used up or spent

protons tiny particles with positive charge, found in the nucleus (central part) of an atom

secondary cell an electrical cell or battery that can be recharged, by putting electricity into it, to change its chemicals back into their original condition

semiconductor substances that carry electric current well or poorly, depending on conditions, such as nearby magnetic fields

series circuit an electric circuit in which the components are connected one after another, in a linear sequence, so current flows through them one after another

solenoid a coil of wire, shaped like a tube with a central long hole

static electricity (electrostatic charge) electrical energy that tends to stay still or static, unless given a route by which to move

superconducors substances that have virtually no resistance to electric currents

transformer device for increasing (or decreasing) the voltage (strength) of electricity, while, at the same time, decreasing (or increasing) its current (quantity)

volts unit measuring the strength or pushing force of an electric current

Books

DiSpezio, Michael A.
Awesome Experiments in Electricity &
Magnetism.
Sterling, 2006

Bridgman, Roger and Challoner, Jack.
Eyewitness: Electronics.
DK Eyewitness Books (series).
Dorling Kindersley, 2000

Parker, Steve.
Fully Charged: Electricity.
Everyday Science (series).
Heinemann, 2005

Parker, Steve.
Opposites Attract: Magnetism.
Everyday Science (series).
Heinemann, 2005

Parker, Steve and Buller, Laura.
Eyewitness: Electricity
DK Eyewitness Books (series).
Dorling Kindersley, 2005

Web sites

HowStuffWorks
www.howstuffworks.com/motor.htm
science.howstuffworks.com/maglev-train.
  htm
The HowStuffWorks sites have many inside
stories on electrical and magnetic machines
and gadgets.

Magnetic Compass
www.navis.gr/navaids/compass.htm
About the magnetic compass, how it works
and its use through the ages in navigation.

Electromagnets
www.schoolscience.co.uk/content/3/
  physics/copper/index.html
Pages about electromagnets, how they work
and what they are used for.

General Energy Timeline
www.eia.doe.gov/kids/history/timelines/
  general.html
A big timeline about energy, especially
making and using electrical energy, with
linked pages that focus more on electricity.

Electricity
www.eia.doe.gov/kids/energyfacts/sources/
  electricity.html
A secondary energy source describes how
electricity is made, moved, and measured.

Alliant Energy Kids: Energy Inventors
www.powerhousekids.com/stellent2/
  groups/public/documents/pub/
  phk_eb_001476.hcsp
Inventors of electrical devices.

How Electricity Is Made
www.dairynet.com/kids/electric.html
Generating electricity at the power plant
and delivering it to homes and other users,
including a virtual tour of a power plant.

WITHDRAWN

alloys, 16
alternating current (AC), 35, 36, 37, 38
amber, 6
Ampère, André-Marie, 17
amps, 17
analog technology, 41, 42
animal electricity, 6, 7
anodes, 19
armatures, 30, 31, 32
artificial limbs, 9
atoms, 6, 9, 16, 24, 25

bar magnets, 25
Bardeen, John, 42
batteries, 5, 6, 18, 19, 20, 21
blackouts, 5
Brattain, Walter, 42
bullet trains, 31

capacitors, 13, 40
cathodes, 19
cell phones, 4, 40, 41
circuits, 17, 18, 19, 20, 21, 22, 23, 40, 41
Colombus, Christopher, 7
commutators, 31, 32
conductors, 16, 17, 18, 19
copper, 16, 23
Coulomb, Charles de, 15
crop-dusters, 15
crystals, 22

digital technology, 41, 43
direct current (DC), 35, 36
domains, 24, 25
domestic electricity, 39
dry cells, 19, 21

Edison, Thomas, 36
electric cells, 6, 18, 19
electric currents, 12, 35, 36

electric motors, 4, 29, 30, 31, 32, 33, 36
electrical discharges, 6, 12
electricity grids, 34, 35, 36
electricity in animals, 6, 7
electricity sources, 39
electrocardiograms, 8
electroencephalograms (EEG), 8, 9
electrolytes, 19, 21, 23
electromagnetic induction, 36, 37
electromagnetic spectrum, 42, 43
electromagnetism, 5, 28, 29, 30, 31
electromagnets, 28, 29, 30, 31
electronics, 40, 41, 42, 43
electrons, 6, 10, 11, 12, 19, 24, 25
electroplating, 23
electrostatic charges, 12, 13, 14, 15, 26
energy efficiency, 33

Faraday, Michael, 30
filaments, 18
fossil fuels, 38
Franklin, Benjamin, 13

Galvani, Luigi, 18
gamma rays 42
generating electricity, 34, 35, 36, 37, 38
generators, 13, 15, 34, 35, 36, 37, 38, 39
geographic poles, 26, 27
Gilbert, William, 27
Greeks, ancient, 11
greenhouse gases, 39

Henry, Joseph, 30

infrared rays, 42
insulators, 16
integrated circuits, 40

iron, 25, 28, 29

kinetic energy, 31, 36

left-hand rule, 33
Leyden jar, 13
lightning, 6, 12,
lightning rods, 12
lodestone, 24, 26

magnetic compasses, 26, 32
magnetic Earth, 26, 27
magnetic fields, 25, 26, 27, 28, 29
magnetic poles, 25, 26, 27, 30, 31
magnetite, 24
microchips, 40, 41, 43
microwaves, 5, 42
muscles, 7, 8

nervous systems, 8, 9
neutrons, 10

Ohm, Georg Simon, 17
ohms, 17
Ørsted, Hans Christian, 32

parallel circuits, 22, 23

photocopiers, 14
power plants, 34, 35, 36, 37, 38, 39
primary cells, 21
protons, 10, 11

radio waves, 5, 42
rechargeable batteries, 21
right-hand rule, 33
rotors, 36, 37

Saint Elmo's Fire, 7
secondary cells, 21
semiconductors, 40
series circuits, 21, 22
sharks, 7
Shockley, William, 42
simple circuits, 17, 18
solenoid, 28
speed of light, 10

static electricity, 12, 13, 14, 15
stators, 36, 37
superconductors, 17

Tesla, Nikola, 25, 35, 36
teslas, 25
Thales of Miletus, 11
thunderstorms, 6, 7
transformers, 30, 38, 39
transistors, 40, 41, 42
tubes, 41

ultraviolet, rays, 42

Van de Graff, Robert, 15
Volta, Alessandro, 17, 20
volts, 8, 15, 17, 38, 39

X-rays, 42